Opening the Third Eye: Master the Ability to Increase Intuition; Develop Higher Levels of Awareness and Consciousness, and Stronger Spiritual

Connection by Unlocking the Power of the Pineal Gland

By S.J. Morgan

Free Bonus Gift

As a special thank you for downloading and purchasing this book, I would like to offer you an exclusive free eBook about the "Law of Attraction 101" which I believe can personally help anybody achieve their dreams.

If you want to take your life to another level, and become the ultimate manifester and truly learn the stepping blocks of mastering the law of attraction, then this guide book will help tremendously.

In this free eBook, you will learn the 25 little steps that can bring you massive results.

>>> DOWNLOAD THIS FREE EBOOK BY CLICKING HERE<<<

Law of Attraction 101

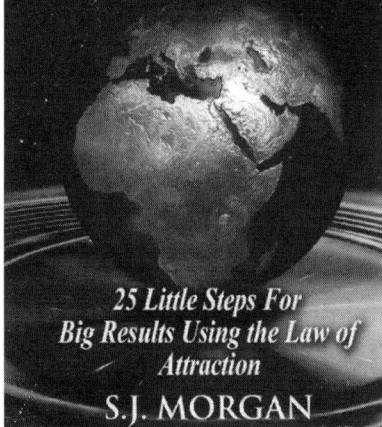

25 Little Steps For Big Results Using the Law of Attraction

S.J. MORGAN

Table of Contents

Introduction

The world of health care is more interested in natural ways to cure an individual rather than medicines and injections. No matter how much we claim these medicines and injections to be safe and secure, some of them do have side effects in the long run. Moreover, when you are living a healthy life with a staple diet, exercise, and meditation you will automatically notice the difference.

Organic food items with regular exercise and meditation will give you a sense of happiness and inner peace. The modern day researchers have time and again highlighted how the glands of the endocrine system play a significant role towards our well being and happiness.

Our endocrine system is comprised of a series of glands that secrete specific hormones in our blood stream. These hormones in turn give signals to the different cells of the body so that there is proper growth and development, metabolism rate, tissue function, and mood swings.

When one is able to fully develop the pituitary and pineal glands through meditation and concentration, upon the sixth and the seventh chakras, their vibrations will activate the third eye. And it is through this third eye that we can connect with the spiritual side of existence. It is through this third eye that we will be able to elevate ourselves from the normal material things of life and feel one with the Superior Being.

This wondrous part of our body, namely the Pineal Gland, is also known by several names. Popular among them is the epiphysis cerebri, epiphysis, conarium, or the "Third Eye." Located near the center of the brain, this hormone resembles a tiny pinecone, and hence this name. Although hidden deep inside the brain, this hormone has been an object of desire of many mystery schools and religions across the globe.

This pea shape hormone plays an important role in the writings of Pythagoras and Plato. In fact, one will also find it being mentioned in the Egyptian scripts and Roman Catholic Church writings. Over the years, different research studies have been conducted, different writings have been published, and different exercises have been recommended to make the third eye active. But without dedication, commitment, and the desire to connect with the Spiritual side, one will not be able to accomplish anything.

In the average person, the pineal gland is dormant and atrophied, [calcified]. In this book, we will discuss in detail:

- What is the Third Eye?
- Benefits of the Third Eye
- Evidence behind the theory of the Third Eye
- Is opening the Third Eye worth the effort?
- Steps on how to open the Third Eye (multiple ways)
- Steps on how to close the Third Eye

The book aims to give you an in-depth and complete idea about how the pineal gland functions, and how we can master the Third Eye if we aim to increase our intuition, develop higher levels of awareness and consciousness, and establish a stronger spiritual connection. A comprehensive book, this one will provide answers to many of your questions that have been bothering you for years!

What Is the Third Eye?

The Third Eye is the 6th Chakra of our body, and is linked with our "sixth sense." Most of us are more familiar with the concept of the sixth sense than the word "Anja," another name of the Third Eye.

This Chakra connects us with our internal intuitions, and plays a significant role for our sharp senses, the ability to predict the future and being able to perceive the nonverbal messages, in other words "telepathy." Often people with an enhanced Third Eye can perceive the future, and even receive messages from the past

Representing Color: Purple is associated with this 6th Chakra.

Location of the Chakra in the Body: in the centre of the forehead, between the eyes.

Main element of this Chakra: Light is associated with this chakra. Although the Third Eye is blind, it boasts of a deep vision inside. It helps to connect the conscious with the unconscious part of the mind.

Characteristics of this 6th Chakra: When the Third Eye is in balance, you will experience an all round development where you will experience empathy for others, higher intellect, and concentration. You will be able to differentiate between reality and imagination. Logic and emotion will be predominant.

When this chakra is imbalanced, we experience sleep problems, fatigue, day dreaming, lack of concentration, and a prevailing sense of disorientation.

How to Balance This Chakra

- Meditation is a great way to develop and nurture your intuition.
- Aromatic essential oils such as Myrrh, Olibanum and even Patchouli are great for developing concentration.
- Try and use the color purple in your daily life. Say for example, wear a purple scarf or a purple top so as to increase the flow of energy.
- Opt for soothing classical music that will enable the flow of positive energy in your body.
- Amethyst, tanzanite, and tourmaline are popular stones that are associated with the Third Eye ,and you can easily wear them to balance the 6th chakra.
- Seek answers to questions that have been bugging you for a long time. Seek the answers from the Universe. You may to wait for a few seconds to several months before the answer is delivered to you. The answer can come from within as well, or there may be signs or incidents happening that will give answers to your questions.
- Keep a diary where you need to write down the dreams and visions that you are experiencing.
- Close your eyes, and let your body relax. Remain in this position for several minutes until you feel the external muscles relax around your eyes. Then slowly soften the muscles inside your eyes, allowing the sense of relaxation to penetrate deep inside your body. Try and notice the images appearing in your mind's eye.

- Try your hand at drawing. Or opt for another form of art that requires a high level of concentration and observation on your part.
- Try out star gazing.
- Repeat positive thoughts such as:

"My imagination is clear and vivid."

"My mind is agile and powerful."

"I have strong intuition and insight."

"I see and understand the bigger picture."

"My intellect is strong and useful."

"I envision good and positive images."

"I am open to the wisdom inside me."

"Greater spiritual awareness awaits me."

How to Make the Most of Your 6th Chakra

Use Light: As light is the main element of this chakra, try and use light to improve the flow of good and positive energy around you. This can be done in several ways. Spend as much time as possible in the sunlight. Watch the sunlight bounce off through water, or gaze at the sunlight through the tree leaves. Spend hours gazing at the stars and the moon. Surround yourself with bright lights at your home and office. If required, change the light and adjust it so that there is strong light around you.

Soak up Knowledge: Look for knowledge from anything and everything around you. Treat every incident as a teacher, and seek knowledge from it. Some incidents will make you aware of the bad things, while others will associate you with the good things prevailing around you. Don't underestimate any knowledge. Channelize the information collected to clear your mind from doubts, fears, and confusions. You should soak up knowledge at all possible times and situations.

Trust your Intuition: Our intuition is our best teacher and advisor. Listen to your intuition at all the times. If something does not feel right, then don't do it, even if it would mean a loss of material wealth. Your inner peace and happiness are more important. Spend some time with yourself. Listen to your inner voice. Hear what it has to say. You will get answers to many things out of this silence. Be receptive of this silence.

Follow Your Natural Flow of Energy: Do what your body permits you to do, and do not over exert yourself. Eat only when you are hungry. If you feel sleepy, then take adequate rest. If you want to do something, do it. Listen to your body and its symptoms. Pay attention. Don't do something that you have no interest in.

Vision Board: What are you aims and aspirations? Make a vision board where you should jot down your aspirations. Try and seek these aims and aspirations. Fix the timeframe within which you plan to achieve it. Stick to the plan to make it a resounding success. Don't give up. Concentration and determination matters the most.

Opt for Eye Exercises: There are several eye exercises that you can try out. Practice them at home. Over a period of time, you will be able to master these exercises and achieve the desired level of concentration so that your Third Eye awakens for that spiritual uplifting.

Benefits of the Third Eye

If someone posed the question "how many eyes do you have?" most of us would reply that we have two eyes. But the answer is incorrect. All of us possess the Third Eye. However, many of us are unaware of it and even if we have heard about it, we still don't have a clear idea about how to use it properly so that all the benefits are derived.

Our Third Eye is invisible, but it is as present as the rest of the two eyes. This Third Eye is the source of all intuition, wisdom, overall growth and development, inner peace, and happiness. Our Third Eye gives us an insight into the past, forewarning of the future, and a better understanding of the present. So what are the potent benefits of this Third Eye? Let us unravel:

- Our Third Eye knows the unknown, and can see the unseen. This 6th chakra is a potent source of information that can act as a guide and teacher as and when the time arises. There are times when you must have experienced that someone is watching you, but when you turned around there was no one there. We all have our angels and guardians guiding and protecting us. Have you ever felt that your loved one was in danger and a few minutes later, you received a call justifying your worst fears? All of us, regardless of our gender have a powerful and unique "sixth sense" that tends to give us symptoms and signals if anything unwanted is going to happen.

- All that we need to know is within ourselves. The moment that we open up our Third Eye via meditation, we will get the answers to all our queries. There is no need of a crystal ball or tarot cards to seek the answers of the unknown. Once you start meditating, you will be able to channelize the positive energy inside you and will get in touch with your inner being. Slowly but surely, you will experience inner peace and happiness. Your satisfaction will no longer depend on materialistic things. You will be happy anywhere, irrespective of the circumstance or the situation.

- You will get in touch with your inner intuitive wisdom. Through meditation, you will get in touch with the higher stages of consciousness, and you will become self aware and will be able to keep your stress at bay, control your emotions, and use this intuition for the greater good. As you will be in touch with your present and can foresee the future, you will be able to guide yourself so that all the negative energy is sucked out of your system and that positive energy flows all around you. As you meditate and become aware of your intelligence and wisdom, you will be aware of the inner strength that you possess.

- The moment that you have opened your third eye, you will open a world of endless possibilities where advanced consciousness will be at your fingertips. You will not only be aware of the different levels of consciousness and realms, but you will develop a sense of passion for the present and the future. When you will develop your concentration and dedication through meditation, you will be able to release anxiety and stress from your daily life. You will no longer be bogged down by your unpaid electricity bill, or that fact that you need to make an impressive presentation the next day. The confidence that you have gathered will help you face the challenges head on, and you will be able to sail smoothly through any situation.

- Negative thoughts will become a problem of the past. We all are humans, and it is natural for us to be stressed and tensed. And when we are tensed, we experience negative thoughts that affect our performance and growth. But with the opening of the third eye, you will able to develop your inner peace and strength, and hence the negative thoughts will come and go. They will not occupy any place in your life any more.

- Through meditation, you will be able to enjoy the sights, sounds, and visions that were earlier unimagined. Use this sense of development and inner growth for your inner peace and well being. Become an observer of the unseen, and collect information from everything that is happening around you. Develop your intellect, common sense, power of observation, and use these insights for attaining spiritual growth.

- In order to know what is out there, you need to look inside. For every question that we have, the answer lies within. Through meditation, you will get all the answers from within. Just give time. If you have worries like should you change the job, where should you relocate, when should you get married – look for all the answers from within you. You might get the answer in a few minutes, or it might take months. But listen to your intuition. You will never go wrong.

The moment one is able to awaken the Third Eye, he will be able to develop his sense of intuition as well as sixth sense. The positive energy created can be used to achieve different aims. One cannot overlook the sense of dedication, commitment, and the feeling of inner peace and happiness that occurs when you awaken the Third Eye in order to achieve the different benefits.

And it is through this Third Eye that we can connect with the spiritual side of existence. It is through this Third Eye that we will be able to elevate ourselves from the normal material things of life, and feel one with the Superior Being.

Evidence Behind the Theory of the Third Eye

The concept of "Third Eye" is not something new. It is an age-old concept. If we flip through the pages of history, we will come across many chapters where the existence of the "Third Eye" has been mentioned time and again. You will find it in animals such as the ancient tuataras or iguanas of New Zealand. If we go by the different research studies across the generations, we can safely say that there is a high possibility that the Third eEe is nature's first eye, especially in case of the vertebrates and man. However, the mystery shrouding the role and function of the pineal gland is still not clear.

If we take the scientific explanations, then it is made up of cells that have distinct and unique features which are very similar to the light sensitive cells found in the retina. Hence, we can safely say that this organ is related to the power of sight. This gland receives signals from the brain, and gives signals to the optic nerves. This pea shaped gland secretes the hormone melatonin, which plays a significant role in the circadian rhythms or the sleep/wake cycle.

Let us consider the Theosophical literature aspect. This literature emphasizes that in addition to the physiological functions, this gland also plays an important role as the psycho-physiological center or the 6th chakra which is involved with intuition, the sixth sense.

The world of myths and mysteries are no less. They have their own explanations. They have their own concepts regarding the evolution of human civilization and the importance of the Third Eye. If you read through the story of the Ulysses fights, you will fight the mention of the one eyed giant Cyclops of Greece. In Hinduism, you will find the mention of the Third Eye as part of the mystical eye of Siva which stands for direct cosmic vision and intuition. These timeless folklores tell stories about how mankind came into existence and the different battles fought.

If we check out the writings and information collected on the primitive ages, we will see that the Third Eye was very much in existence even before the two eyes were formed and became dominant in the later stages. Interestingly, both the two eyes and the pineal gland form out of the tissue layers present in the embryonic brain.

Biology recognizes the pineal gland as nature's first eye, at least in the case of the most primitive vertebrates. Over the centuries, vertebrates and invertebrates have developed eyes of different kinds. This Third Eye is prevalent in the case of fishes, amphibians, and reptiles. One can also find this gland in the birds as well.

Paleontologists claim that dinosaurs had the Third Eye. They are of the opinion that if you see the opening in the skull, you can make out the presence of an eye out there. The later stages of dinosaurs, especially the mammal-like dinosaurs, had these eyes as well, but over the years the eye got receded under the skull and turned into the pineal gland that is found in man and other vertebrates.

There are many who question the existence of God. They are against the belief that God and the human kingdoms gave birth to the plant kingdom and the lower animals rather than the opposite scenario. As per the theospic descriptions, the human being did not come into existence from an end-on transformation of body types. On the contrary, it was the angels who gave birth to the astral models that later on became human beings.

The earliest forms of pre-humans were spiritual beings who had a higher vision and could see the ethereal planes. You may believe in this concept or may not. But don't forget that the earth went through several stages of cooling before it turned into the solid form. So the theospic explanation could be valid.

As per H. P. Blavatsky, in the early stages of the third root race, the physical nature was more of a plastic kind compared to the present day form. More than 18 million years ago, these developments, in culmination with the consciousness factor, led to the formation of the psychological aspect which aimed to perfect the human brain through its association with the physical nature of the brain. This in turn led to the growth of different senses in a more refined way.

As per the Norse mythology, God Odin had to sacrifice one of his eyes so that he could drink from the well of Wisdom. He went ahead and sacrificed the Third Eye. Read through the story of Adam and Eve, and you will find references to the historical evolution of mankind and how with the passage of time, man lost his touch with the Third Eye as he became more and more involved with the daily chores and the materialist things in his life. As he failed to make use of his Third Eye, it became dormant over the years and gradually receded.

Every phase of growth and evolution reflects its set of wisdom and intelligence. It is up to us to activate our Third Eye, and channelize it so that we can surround ourselves with positive energy. If we are looking for inner peace and happiness and want to develop our intuition and sixth sense, then we have no option but to turn to the awakening of the Third Eye.

Even today, the pea shaped pineal gland is the source of our intuition and awareness level. Whenever we have a hunch about something, this gland starts to vibrate gently, which in turn lead to our intuition about the particular incident.

As we begin the journey for spiritual growth and development, we have to monitor and balance our energies so that the awakening of the Third Eye becomes possible. The best and the most effective way to master the art is by practicing unselfish qualities of character and intuition in our daily activities so that, with the passage of time, we can awaken and control our Third Eye.

Is Opening the Third Eye Worth the Effort?

The Third Eye or the pineal gland deals with our sixth sense. By now, you know that all of us are born with the sixth sense. But in most of the cases it remains dormant. We are not even aware of it. There is a high chance that you were not aware of it before you stumbled across this book. But yes, it is true; all of us have the 6th Chakra in us. And when you awaken the 6th Chakra, you will be able to notice a difference in your life.

In the initial days, you might experience a headache or your head might appear to be heavy with a buzzing sound. But a few days later, when your body gets attuned to the 6th Chakra, all these symptoms will vanish. Due to lack of knowledge on this subject, many think that opening the Third Eye will be destructive. But it is not so. It all depends on how you channelize the energy around you.

The main aim of awakening the Third Eye is to enhance and heighten your senses. This will in turn get your body in sync with the spiritual beings around you. Our guiding angels are always there with us. But we don't realize it.

When you open the pineal gland, you will be able to feel their existence. In fact, you will be able to see them. As already mentioned in the previous chapter, starting from the prehistoric age to the present day, there are different write-ups on this. Researchers have explained in different ways how the Third Eye is an integral part of us.

Is It Worth Awakening Your Third Eye?

Our Third Eye helps to open up our intuition, inner peace, happiness, mental peace, overall growth, and development. Forget about all this; take into account the hectic lifestyle that we are leading. In this scenario, when you awaken your pineal gland you are getting attuned to the higher spiritual beings and, as such, are able to experience a sense of calmness and confidence.

As stated earlier, you need to channelize the energy in the right direction. But beware, do not over do anything. Maintain a balance between your spiritual journey and your physical existence. Otherwise, your heightened senses might over power you and you will lose track of your physical existence.

If you fail to maintain the balance, you might experience discomfort and uneasiness. It may happen that you might find that too many thoughts are running through your mind, and that it is too much for you in case if you fail to handle it.

The visions are nothing but you becoming aware of the beings around you. You will be able to see them the moment that you close your eye. You can also see bright lights flashing in front of you. All these visions will make you aware of the spiritual world around us. So channelize your energy in the right direction.

Often, it will happen that you are having dreams that have no connection with your present life. Maintain a diary, and jot down all that you have seen. In the initial days, it will not be possible to remember all the details. Slowly but steadily, you will be able to remember the remotest detail of the dreams. These dreams are nothing but premonitions of what is going to happen in the future.

Even "de ja vu" is a sense of the Third Eye awakening.

You think that the incident has happened before, so why is it taking place again? Well, your sixth sense had pre-warned you about the happening. But the daily activities in our life made your forget all about it. so when it really took place, you had a feeling of being there before as well.

One of the most common ways to awaken the Third Eye is through meditation (as you will come to know in the following chapters). We all know that a few minutes of meditation have not harmed anyone. In fact, it will increase your concentration and your overall performance.

The word "AUM" is a universal sound that is associated with the universal vibrations. When you chant this word, you are getting attuned to the universe and its mysticism. Concentrate on the throbbing of the pineal gland located in-between your brows; you will notice a change in your existence.

All that you see around you is pulsating with energy and vibration. Nothing is standing still, even for a second.

Everything has a motion. Even an inanimate object like stone, when it rolls down creates a motion in its journey. When we chant the word "AUM," there is a vibration that has a frequency of 432 Hz. And surprisingly, all the vibrational frequency in this wide Universe has the same frequency!!

As a result this word ("AUM") can be considered to be the basic sound of the Universe. So when you are chanting this word, you are actually acknowledging the existence of all other beings in the nature – both physical and spiritual.

So when you are awakening your pineal gland, you are actually having a profound influence on your physical existence, as this will help to calm down your nervous system and will help you to get rid of tension, stress, and will also decrease your blood pressure, which in turn will improve your heart's condition.

Awakening the Third Eye teaches us to take care of ourselves and helps us to realize the purpose of our existence. You will feel calm even in the midst of a crowd.

As stated in the first chapter, repeat positive thoughts such as:

"My imagination is clear and vivid."

"My mind is agile and powerful."

"I have strong intuition and insight."

"I see and understand the bigger picture."

"My intellect is strong and useful."

"I envision good and positive images."

"I am open to the wisdom inside me."

"Greater spiritual awareness awaits me."

Unfortunately, it is not possible to master the art of awakening the eye within a fortnight. It will require time, effort, dedication, commitment, and the desire to achieve it, and that too on a regular basis.

In the following chapters, you will learn how to awaken your pineal gland and how to close it. But the question remains: is it really worth the effort? If the different research studies and writings are anything to go by, then awakening the pineal gland is a good thing, as it will give the required purpose in life.

Don't forget that human beings are a part of the Universe as well. We have a duty towards it as well. And we have been created to maintain the balance in the entire universe.

Let the following chapters in the books help you make your call whether you would like to awaken your Third Eye or not. Even if you decide against it, you will have collected knowledge on a subject that was practically unknown to you.

Steps on How to Open the Third Eye (Multiple Ways)

For a long time, the role played by the pineal gland remained unacknowledged by biology, but if you take into account the mystical traditions, you will come across writings where they have mentioned the presence of this gland in the middle of the brain. In fact, they have also highlighted how this gland is the link between the physical and the spiritual world.

In your journey towards spiritual attainment, it is important that you "awaken" your Third Eye. This is essential if you wish to raise your frequency and higher consciousness through the Third Eye. Our sixth sense or the Third Eye, as it is popularly known, has been seen as the most powerful and potent source of ethereal energy available to mankind, and it is because of this that we consider this gland to be the gateway that leads to the inner world of consciousness and intuition. So how does one activate it?

Meditation is the most popular means. Visualization yoga comes a close second that allows an individual to see beyond the physical.

The list of the benefits and abilities of the pineal gland include clarity, concentration, intuition, decisiveness, calmness, insight, inner peace, and happiness in addition to:

- Vivid and crystal clear dreams.
- Better and refined astral projections.
- Sound sleep.
- Heightened imagination.
- Feeling the presence of beings around you, seeing things with eyes closed, enhancing aura viewing.
- Ability to feel positive energy in a more effective manner.

How to Purify and Activate Your Third Eye

- **Learning how to meditate:** Find a place that is quite and cozy, so that you can sit and meditate without being disturbed. Now sit on the ground with your legs crossed. In case you are not comfortable sitting on the ground, then sit on a chair. Keep your back straight, your head high, and don't let your shoulders slouch.

  Most of us hold some sort of tension within us that we are unaware of. When you sit down to meditate, you will realize this. So relax your body, let your muscles relax, and move your head from side to side to loosen your body. Now you need to concentrate. This is perhaps the most difficult part. It is not possible to achieve absolute concentration at the first attempt. When you try to concentrate, you will see that different thoughts are trickling down your mind. Don't fight them, but don't give in as well.

- **Opening up Your Intuitive Side:** Many people who claim to be introverts have a better understanding of the people around them. As they converse less, they observe people more. Hence, they are a better judge of character. They tend to pick up on body language, facial expressions, sarcasm and so on. Wondering how this will help you?

  Visit a restaurant all by yourself, order some food, and sit and observe the people around you. Try to listen to the conversation going on around you. Don't snoop, but try to hear. From the conversations, try to imagine different stories about them. Slowly, you will pick up the art and will be able to imagine better stories.

The next time that you are part of a family get together, just sit and enjoy your food. Don't take part in the conversation. Observe how the others are reacting to the topic being discussed. See how the non-speakers are reacting to the conversation. A little bit of practice, and you will slowly but surely develop your intuitive qualities.

- **Pay attention to your dreams:** Most people with psychic   powers believe that dreams serve as a premonition of something that is going to happen in the future. So play close attention to your dreams. Try to recollect them in the morning. See how much you can remember. A few weeks down, you will notice that you are able to remember almost all of the dreams that you saw the previous night.

- **Listen to your gut instincts:** Did you ever experience a peculiar feeling about a person, place, or incident? And did you experience these feelings without any strong evidence? These feelings are termed to be the result of a gut instinct. Unfortunately, most of us tend to overlook this. The next time you have these feelings pay attention.

However, if a person is not taking care of their pineal gland, all this intuitive energy will be cut off from him/her. This is referred to as the calcification of the Third Eye. Most of us undergo this calcification process by the time we turn 17 years of age. In fact, this process can be so severe that if you undergo an MRI scan, you will see the formation of calcium lumps. However, there is good news. There are ways by which you can re-open your Third Eye.

- **Avoid Fluoride**: Avoid tap water as much as you can. They have fluoride in them. In fact, the fluoridated toothpaste is no good either. If possible, avoid cooking your food with this water as well.

- **Start Using Essentials Oils**: Make essential oils a part of your daily life. Good choices include lavender, sandalwood, and pine. You can inhale them directly, or add it in your bathing water as well.

- **Try Sun gazing**: Try this for at least 15 minutes regularly. But make sure that you don't do it in the middle of the day, as your eye will be badly affected. Do it during sunrise and sunset.

- **Collect Crystals**: There are some specific crystals that can be used to decalcify the pineal gland. Amethyst, laser quartz, moonstone, and purple sapphire are the crystals that you can opt for.

- **Massage with Magnets**: Attach a piece of a magnet with adhesive between your brows. Magnets when attached with the body create alkaline which will help to decalcify the pineal gland. Do this when you are awake for a few minutes every day.

As with everything else, there is no fixed rule that all these work for all individuals. You can opt for all these or a mixture to find out what works best for you. However, you have to be dedicated and committed enough, and carry out all these steps if you really want to open / re-open your Third Eye.

Steps on How to Close the Third Eye!

So your efforts to open your Third Eye are working well, and you are making progress as well. You are experiencing that tingling sensation, and seeing things from the corner of your eyes. Your intuition has developed, and you seem to assess situations. All this is quite exciting. However, there is a small glitch.

All of these things are happening at once, and you are a bit overwhelmed. So what can you do to shut it down? If you think that you need to slow down the process and that the tone of your psychic awareness should be steady but at a slower pace, then it may be that too much energy is passing through your Third Eye or the 6th chakra. Just because you have awakened the Third Eye for only a few days and too much time has not passed, everything seems to be running wild. Here are a few steps by which you can close the Third Eye.

Complete closure or the global close: Imagine your body and how it felt and reacted to happenings around it before the 6th chakra was open. For this, you need to sit down, relax, and think of the particular incident, remembering how you felt at that particular point of time. The trick lies in remembering how you felt at that moment of time.

Now try and feel the same thing. If you do it correctly, you will feel relaxed at once. In order to feel the previous feelings, you have to forcefully close your chakra so that your body is not attuned to the higher consciousness anymore. For this, you need absolute dedication and commitment. You cannot give up midway. Imagine your chakra getting closed slowly, and your body returning to the state when the Third Eye was not awakened. It will take time, but over a period of time you will be able to do it.

The Snap: This is more of an instant reaction, just like the way you snap out of a daydream, you need to snap out of the awakening. Pull down your skull cap. You will feel it directly above your head, and you must pull it directly onto your head before you close shut the Third Eye. It is a true process where you need to physically shut the chakra.

Once you feel that the chakra is closed, it will be closed. Don't give in unless the chakra is closed. Say to yourself that the chakra will not open, never ever. Go back to the time when your body had not witnessed the awakening. Feel that particular state of mind in order to snap out of the heightened senses.

Don't give in: When you are trying to close the Third Eye, the beings around you will trick you into thinking that the Third Eye is still open. Don't give in to the existence of the beings or to what they are trying to convey. Many experience the beings interfering in their process to close down the chakra. There is nothing to get stressed about.

Just don't give in. The beings will give you the impression that the senses have become light by placing energy on the chakra, but don't believe them. You have closed it, and that's the truth. Once you have got the system protected, maintain it. Believe that you have closed the system, and take a nap. When you get a proper sleep, everything will get back to its place.

Get Out of Your Head and Out of Your Third Eye

Just like the way that you have devoted time and attention in awakening your Third Eye, in the same way devote time towards your daily activities. Be in touch with your regular life. This will help you to maintain the balance. Your Third Eye cannot remain completely open at all the times if you keep your brain engaged elsewhere. So always divide your attention in such a way that you are able to carry out all the regular activities.

How to do this:

- Pay attention to the other details in your life. If your house is full of dirt, dust, and grim, then pay attention to organizing them.
- Pay attention to your finances: pay your bills and clear all your dues on time. Have a set monthly budget, and try to stick to it by all means.
- Opt for different exercises, even if it is a walk, then go for it.

- Get a massage done.

Maintain a normal lifestyle: No matter how much time you give to your spiritual awakening, do not ignore your physical existence. Remember that closing the Third Eye is not that easy, and cannot be done by a quick fix method. If you want to ensure that too many thoughts don't run through your mind throughout the day or you don't want to have visualizations as and when they take place, then you need to balance your life. You are not an object that you will shift from one place to another without any repercussions. So in order to avoid all this mess, channelize your energy properly and in the right direction.

If none of these steps work for you and there are different kinds of thoughts running up and down in your mind and it is hampering your daily activities, then take a bath with sea salts or Epsom salt in it. Let your body soak in the warmth, and release all the energy collected over the days. This will help you to relax your muscles, and you will get relief for the time being. But keep in mind that it is a temporary measure.

As we have already stated in the previous chapter, there is no definite and absolute way by which you can open or close your Third Eye. What works for one individual might not work for the other. But what you can do is mix and match the different steps to see what works best for you.

Frequently Asked Questions

Q. What is the Third Eye?

A. The Third Eye is the 6th Chakra of our body, and is linked with our "sixth sense.". Most of us are more familiar with the concept of the sixth sense than the word "Anja," another name of the Third Eye. The Chakra connects us with our internal intuitions and plays a significant role for our sharp senses, the ability to predict the future, and being able to perceive the non-verbal messages, in other words "telepathy." Often, people with an enhanced Third Eye can perceive the future, and even receive messages from the past.

The color purple is associated with this 6th Chakra.

Q. How can I open my Third Eye?

A. Meditation is the most popular means. Visualization yoga comes a close second that allows an individual to see beyond the physical.

Q. What are the benefits of the Third Eye?

A. Our Third Eye is invisible, but it is as present as the rest of the two eyes. This Third Eye is the source of all intuition, wisdom, overall growth and development, inner peace, and happiness. Our Third Eye gives us an insight of the past, forewarning of the future, and a better understanding of the present.

The list of the benefits and abilities of the pineal gland include clarity, concentration, intuition, decisiveness, calmness, insight, inner peace, and happiness, in addition to:

- Vivid and crystal clear dreams.
- Better and refined astral projections.
- Sound sleep.
- Heightened imagination.
- Feeling the presence of beings around you, seeing things with eyes closed, and enhancing aura viewing.

- Ability to feel positive energy in a more effective manner.

In order to know what is out there, you need to look inside. For every question that we have, the answer lies within. Through meditation, you will get all the answers from within. Just give it time.

Q. How can it affect my health?

A. Awakening the Third Eye has more positive effects than negative. You experience a sense of inner peace and satisfaction. Your overall happiness improves. However, in order to ensure that no negative effect takes place, you will have to channelize all your energy towards the positive end.

Q. Is the Third Eye related to personal development?

A. The Third Eye can play a significant role in personal development. With your heightened senses, you will be able to experience the unconscious part of the mind, and start your journey towards spiritual uplifting. When you experience inner peace and happiness, your outlook automatically changes, leading to an overall personal development.

Q. Will my professional world be affected?

A. As stated above, the 6th chakra will ensure that you have an overall development in all spheres of your life. The professional world is a part of it.

Q. How can I improve my relationships?

A. With your heightened senses, you will be able to understand whether the opposite person is lying, trying to cheat you or not. You will be a better judge of character, and this will reflected in all the relationships that you share.

Q. Why do I need to awaken my Third Eye?

A. All of us are born with the pineal gland. However, it is up to us whether we would like to awaken our Third Eye or not.

Once you open the Third Eye, you will be able to enjoy all the benefits associated with it. (Already mentioned above).

Q. Where is this done? Is there any specific institute?

A. You can practice this all by yourself, or you can join a meditation centre and under the guidance of a psychic, you can awaken your Third Eye.

Q. What are the risks involved?

A. The risk factor is involved with the way you channelize your thoughts and intuitions. Like everything else, there is a negative side to this as well. If you fail to channelize your visions, thoughts, and intuitions in the right direction, then they can overtake you and affect your lifestyle.

Q. What are the visions all about?

A. The visions are nothing but you becoming aware of the beings around you. You will be able to see them the moment that you close your eye. You can also see bright lights flashing in front of you. All these visions will make you aware of the spiritual world around us.

Q. What if I don't like the experience after awakening the Third Eye?

A. It may happen that you might find that too many thoughts are running through your mind, and that it is too much for you. In case you fail to handle it and if it is affecting your daily life, then opt for the steps that will help you to close your Third eye.

Q. How can I close the Third Eye?

A. There are different ways that you can do it. But the most common way is to maintain a balance between your physical world and your spiritual world. After you have awakened your

Third Eye, don't forget to carry out your daily activities so that the balance is retained.

Q. Will there be any harm done to me if I close my Third Eye, after awakening it?

A. No. There are many individuals who exist who have closed their Third Eye after awakening it.

Q. How much of this is true? And how much is fiction?

A. The concept of the "Third Eye" is not something new. It is an age-old concept. If we flip through the pages of history, we will come across many chapters where the existence of the "Third Eye" has been mentioned time and again.

You will find it in animals such as the ancient tuataras or iguanas of New Zealand. If we go by the different research studies across the generation, we can safely say that there is a high possibility that the Third Eye is nature's first eye, especially in case of the vertebrates and man. However, the mystery shrouding the role and function of the pineal gland is still not clear.

Conclusion

All of us are born with a sixth sense. Some of us make use of it, while others don't pay attention to it. Almost all of us have experienced some sort of premonition or the other. How many times have you experienced that someone is watching you while you are walking on the road but when you turned around there was no one out there? All of us have our own guiding angel looking over us.

With the awakening of the Third Eye, we become aware of them. Our senses get heightened, our intuition develops, and we can see the future, as well as be happy in the present. The Third Eye acts as the gateway between our physical existence and our spiritual world. By now, you have a clear idea about what the Third Eye/ pineal gland / sixth sense means.

The modern day researchers have time and again highlighted how the glands of the endocrine system plays a significant role towards our well being and happiness. Our endocrine system is comprised of a series of glands that secrete specific hormones in our bloodstream. These hormones in turn give signals to the different cells of the body so that there is proper growth and development, metabolism rate, tissue function, and mood swings.

All that we need to know is within ourselves. The moment that we open up our Third Eye via meditation, we will get the answers to all our queries. There is no need of a crystal ball or tarot cards to seek answers of the unknown.

Once you start meditating, you will be able to channelize the positive energy inside you and will get in touch with your inner being. Slowly but surely, you will experience inner peace and happiness. Your satisfaction will no longer depend on materialistic things. You will be happy anywhere, irrespective of the circumstance or the situation.

Check Out Some Of My Other Books

Spirit Guides: Master the Ability to Contact Your Spirit Guides Effortlessly

Psychic: Psychic Development Awaken Your Inner Psychic Abilities

Lucid Dreaming: Complete Guide to Mastering The Art of Lucid Dreams - Improve Creativity, Problem Solving, Confidence & Conquer Your Fears

11313647R00037

Printed in Great Britain
by Amazon.co.uk, Ltd.,
Marston Gate.